# GIFTS OF FOOD

# GIFTS OF FOOD

## Mary Berry

PIATKUS

I have always enjoyed making food presents and receiving them too! Writing this book has been tremendous fun. For helping to make it so my thanks firstly go to Clare Blunt who has, as always, been a power of strength testing and trying the recipes for this book; we have been assisted by Linda Denwood, of Sheffield Polytechnic, who spent part of a six weeks' college placement with us assisting in testing and checking recipes, and proved to be full of good humour and good ideas.

© 1983 Mary Berry

First published in 1983 by
Judy Piatkus (Publishers) Limited
of Loughton, Essex

British Library Cataloguing in Publication Data
Berry, Mary, 1935 –
    Gifts of food
    1. Cookery
    641.5        TX717
    ISBN 0–86188–403–5

Design and drawings by Paul Saunders
Cover designed by Ken Leeder

Typeset by V & M Graphics Ltd, Aylesbury, Bucks
Printed and bound by Mackays of Chatham Ltd

# Contents

# Introduction

A lettuce freshly picked from your own garden, or an elaborate Christmas cake that takes hours to prepare, and bake, and ice.... Presents to eat or drink can be as simple or as complicated as you like to make them. That is the beauty of them. They may not cost much in money but the best ones need a lot of thought and planning to find the right gift for the right person at the right time. A polythene bag of your favourite home-made turkey stuffing is likely to be a better Christmas present for a hard-pressed family cook than the most expensive box of candied fruits. (Do let her know in advance what is coming and so take at least one chore off her mind.)

The best presents are the personal, individual ones, the ones that say this is just for *you*. Food and drink presents give you the opportunity to say just that. After all, everybody has their own particular likes and dislikes. To be given something that you really enjoy, to know that someone has taken the trouble to remember your tastes, adds an extra dimension to the present.

So if you are giving presents from your own kitchen, make them something individual that won't be found on the supermarket shelves. It is worth while studying old-fashioned cookery books to see if you can develop or adapt some of the country recipes that our grandparents used. Perhaps a special recipe has been handed down in your family. Perhaps there is one dish that belongs to your part of the country. Make your own favourites to give as presents: if you and your family enjoy them, the chances are that they will appeal to your friends too.

Remember what people have enjoyed at your house. I find it worth while to keep a note of anything that a guest has specially praised. To have tastes remembered in this way doubles the pleasure in the gift.

There is always a time for giving presents. There are the big festivals like Christmas and Easter, there are the more personal birthdays and anniversaries. There are times when you want to say thank you, or just to show your affection. Food presents can be large or small, expensive or otherwise, solid or liquid. The choice is yours. The only firm rule is to suit the present to the recipient and to the occasion.

## Presentation

If your gift is attractively wrapped, then the pleasure is complete. The child that is in all of us rejoices in a tempting looking parcel, with a colourful wrapping hinting at unimaginable delights inside.

So give a lot of thought to outward appearances, they *are* important. The kind of wrapping you use will depend of course on the contents of the parcel, its size and whether it is to be sent by post or delivered by hand. Collect wrapping materials and containers of different kinds. Save cardboard boxes of all sizes – bought ones can be very expensive. You can often use the base of a box to hold biscuits or small cakes, or sweets, and cover the top with cling film so that the contents are displayed. Then add a bow of bright ribbon.

Ordinary kitchen foil makes a lovely wrapping if used with care. Or wrap the larger parcels in pieces of wallpaper or drawer lining paper. Coloured tissue paper is cheap and effective. Pictures cut from old Christmas cards can be stuck on plain wrapped packets – get the children to help you with this. A home-made Christmas cracker, or a bought one, can be filled with something small and special – a miniature bottle of sloe gin perhaps, or a tiny packet of fudge. Storage jars filled with preserves, terrines holding a pâté, can be given as part of the present.

If you are delivering your parcel by hand, fix a small posy of flowers on top, a sprig of holly for Christmas.

## Labelling

It is important to give plenty of information on the labels on food presents. The friend you are giving to may not be as experienced a cook as you are. Make it clear how long the food can be kept in the fridge, or in the freezer, and give freezing instructions where required. Perhaps a friend is coming out of hospital and you send along a light meal that she and her family can enjoy. Give *full* instructions about heating and serving so that her husband can cope with it. You will take a big weight off her mind.

Label preserves clearly. A typical label might read: *Lemon curd. Store in fridge, use within 6 weeks.* All this helps the recipient. Use a fine tipped waterproof marker pen. Or print the labels with Letraset; this looks very smart and the children enjoy doing it.

Always put the date of making on labels for preserves, pâtés, terrines, pots of cheese, or seafood, or anything that has to be frozen. This should ensure that the food is eaten while it is in prime condition.

## Transporting the parcel

Ideally food presents should be delivered in person. Sometimes they have to be – you could hardly send a basket of fresh eggs through the post. On the other hand, a birthday cake for a son at school at the other end of the country will inevitably go by post, in a good stout box, and at considerable cost. When you deliver by hand you save exorbitant postal charges and need not limit the size of the parcel. Weight and packing are not so important and the present can arrive in all the glory of its bright ribbons and wrapping paper, with flowers on top. Also, you know it has got there safely.

So do think ahead and try to arrange to be in the area in question when presents are due. Keep a calendar of birthdays and anniversaries. Make a trip round friends at Christmas, bringing the parcels along with the Christmas cards. (Allow a good deal of time for this trip, you are sure to be invited in for drinks!)

If you have to post food presents, pay great attention to the packing. Use unbreakable containers. Cakes, biscuits and sweets can travel in airtight tins or plastic freezer boxes. These can then go into a stout cardboard box, packed round with newspaper or wood shavings and covered with strong brown paper, carefully and clearly labelled. Potted foods like pâtés or terrines travel best in foil dishes, but if you are sending these, do remember postal delays, especially at Christmas time. My rule is to post only foodstuffs that keep well and to reserve those breakable jars of preserves or bottles of liqueur for friends to whom I can deliver in person.

## Posting parcels

There is no denying that parcel post is *very* expensive. So when you are planning your parcel, be careful and think of the weight, not forgetting the weight of the packing – and you need lots of packing (see above). Study the current postal rates. Lighter parcels may go more cheaply by letter post. Make sure you send your package off in time for safe and early delivery.

It is worth noting that you can get soft squashy bags from the post office that are very light and are safe and convenient for sending the less delicate presents.

## Timing

Keep an eye on the calendar and consider topical presents. There are the traditional ones, like brandy butter at Christmas, simnel cake for Mothering Sunday, decorated eggs at Easter; these come round every year and the wise cook is ready for them. The cake and Christmas puddings are made in good time, the mincemeat is maturing in the larder, the jars of preserves are lined up on the shelves, the sloe gin is at the peak of perfection. These are the presents that improve with keeping.

There are others that do not. The basket of runner beans picked that morning from your own garden, the bunch of radishes, the bowl of strawberries or raspberries – these are instant presents, to be prepared, given and eaten if possible on the same day.

# BOOZY PRESENTS

These are fun to give, fun to receive, and not usually cheap. A bottle of liqueur whisky for instance would be a *very* special present, but you need not set your sights so high. Miniature bottles are popular Christmas tree gifts. The addition of a little booze does a lot for festive foods.

Even non cooks can score a big success with bought mincemeat, soaked in whisky or brandy and replaced in the jar. Cover the lid with a scrap of cheerful material; if you have used whisky, a bright tartan on top will convey the message.

Sloe gin is easy to make, expensive and much appreciated. If you give it in small bottles a little will go a reasonably long way. I like to save up old medicine bottles for it. You can get new clean corks for the bottles from wine-making shops or large chemists. If you use clear glass bottles the glorious colour of the liquor is almost decoration enough. Add a written label and make it as personal as you can: *specially made by X for Y, with love.*

# Guinness Christmas Pudding

*Makes 2 puddings, each to serve 6–8*

These puddings can be made up to 3 months in advance. Cover the top of the bowls containing the puddings with material (either Christmas fabric or a piece of lightly checked gingham), then they can be boiled as they are, to re-heat for serving.

**12 oz (350 g) fresh white breadcrumbs**
**8 oz (225 g) dark soft brown sugar**
**1 lb (450 g) mixed dried fruit   12 oz (350 g) stoned raisins**
**8 oz (225 g) shredded suet   1 level teaspoon mixed spice**
**grated rind and juice of 1 lemon   ½ pint (300 ml) Guinness**
**2 large eggs, beaten   ¼ pint (150 ml) milk**

**1.** Lightly grease 2 × 2 pint (1 litre) basins. Put the breadcrumbs, sugar, fruit, suet and spice into a large bowl and mix well. Stir in the lemon rind and juice, Guinness, eggs and milk to make a fairly stiff consistency. Divide between the 2 basins and smooth flat. Cover each bowl with a doubled sheet of greaseproof paper and fold a pleat down the centre to allow the pudding to rise. Fasten with string and tie a handle across the top. Refrigerate overnight.

**2.** Next day, using either a steamer or pan with boiling water that comes half-way up the sides of the basins, cook the puddings for 7 hours, topping up with hot water as necessary. When cooked and cooled, replace the original piece of greaseproof paper with fresh, and store in a cool place until required.

# Brandied Apricots

*Makes about 2 x 1lb (450 g) jars*

Quite pricey to make but a special present. Serve with whipped cream or ice cream. Also good to add to fruit salad to give it a kick. Pack in attractive jars that could be part of the present.

**8 oz (225 g) dried apricots**
**8 oz (225 g) caster sugar**
**¼ pint (150 ml) inexpensive brandy**

**1.** Place the apricots in a bowl and cover with cold water, leave to soak overnight. Next day drain off the soaking liquid. Place the apricots in a pan and barely cover with water, bring to the boil, then gently simmer until tender (about 30 minutes).
**2.** Stir in the caster sugar until dissolved. Remove from the heat and when cool add the brandy, transfer to small clean dry jars – wide-necked screw-topped ones are the best. Screw on the lids, label and store in a cool larder. Best to keep at least 1 month before using.

## PRUNES IN GIN

This is a variation of the above recipe. Use 8 oz (225 g) fat good quality prunes instead of the apricots and ¼ pint (150 ml) cheap gin instead of the brandy. Make as above.

# Sloe Gin

*Quantity depends on the amount of sloes*

This is a think-ahead present as the picking time for sloes is August to October according to their ripeness. Sloes are the fruit of the blackthorn bush which has a white flower in spring, and they look like tiny round damsons with the bloom of a black grape. Present in small attractive bottles, clearly labelled.

**fresh sloes**
**gin**
**caster sugar**

**1.** Wash the sloes, remove the stalks and snip each sloe with scissors or a sharp knife. Take clean empty gin bottles, or similar and two-thirds fill with snipped sloes. To each bottle add 8–10 oz (225–275 g) caster sugar and then fill up the bottles with gin. Put the lids on and shake the bottles very well.
**2.** Leave on one side for at least 2 months before using. Shake the bottles about twice a week. In theory you should not drink it for at least 6 months after which time, you should strain the gin from the sloes and discard them. Serve in small glasses as an after dinner drink.

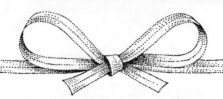

# Liqueur Whisky

*Makes 3 x 8 fl oz (225 ml) bottles*

This recipe came from the director of my last Christmas programme on Thames TV's *Afternoon Plus*. It is remarkably easy and quick to make, and is splendidly smooth and mature tasting. Sadly, you have to start with a bottle of whisky. Honeysmoke essence can be bought from most wine- and beer-making shops. Pack the whisky in small bottles and label neatly.

**1 pint (600 ml) whisky**
**8 oz (225 g) caster sugar**
**3 teaspoons glycerine**
**10 drops honeysmoke essence**

**1.** Put the measured whisky into an empty litre bottle, add the sugar, glycerine and honeysmoke essence. Put on the lid and shake really well to dissolve the sugar.
**2.** Leave overnight and then next day it is ready to drink. Decant into smaller bottles.

# PRESERVES

Jam, jelly, chutney, pickles from your own shelves are always welcome, and doubly so if they are made with your own fruit and vegetables. Jam should be made from fresh fruit – not of course the perfect specimens of strawberries or raspberries that you save for the table, but the smaller ones that may have got a little squashed in the picking. Their flavour is every bit as good. Provided it is in good condition, fruit picked towards the end of its season makes splendid jam, and is often cheaper to buy than earlier in the year. You may like to take advantage of the pick-your-own offers made by local fruit farmers and gather a fine crop at reduced prices.

For chutney you can use windfall apples, provided you cut away the bruised parts. Tomatoes of less than perfect shape, or ones that obstinately refuse to ripen in the garden or on the windowsill go happily into chutney and their flavour is good.

There is nothing difficult about jam making. All you need is a good

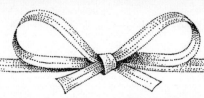

strong preserving pan and a ladle, a supply of fruit and sugar, a reliable recipe and a certain amount of confidence. The rewards are the glorious warm fruity smell in the kitchen and the rows of colourful preserves in the larder. Your friends will be only too glad to share the latter with you.

Before you start, be sure that you have enough jars to put the preserves in. These can be collected throughout the year and friends will probably contribute to the collection if you promise them a pot or two for themselves. Have a supply of different sizes of jar; people living on their own are more likely to welcome two or three small pots of preserve or chutney than the one large one which would delight the mother of a jam-loving family.

When the preserves are potted, seal the jar with waxed paper or Cellophane, or use screw-top jars. The principle of sealing is to exclude all air from the jar. Filling the jar right to the top helps with this.

When the jars are sealed, make them look as attractive as you can. You could, of course, use storage jars which will form part of the present. A circle of gingham or flowered material can cover screw tops. Choose a colour that goes with the preserve, or find a fabric printed with the appropriate fruit – strawberry, apple, peach and so on – and use that to cover the top. Or use a pretty wrapping paper and stick a plain label on it. Labels must be easily legible and should carry the date when the preserve was made.

Pots can travel in boxes, with or without lids, but carefully packed in coloured tissue paper, perhaps with cling film covering the top and showing off the contents. It goes without saying that glass jars of preserves are presents that you deliver in person.

# Lemon Curd

*Fills about 3 × 8 oz (225 g) jars*

Label clearly. Store the curd in the refrigerator and use within 6 weeks. Jams and preserves always look good if they are covered with a lid of pretty material such as gingham.

**4 oz (100 g) butter**
**8 oz (225 g) caster sugar**
**3 lemons**
**3 eggs, beaten**

**1.** Place the butter and sugar in the top of a double saucepan with simmering water in the lower part. If you do not have a double saucepan, use a basin over a pan of water. Stir well until the butter has melted. Stir the finely grated rind and juice from the lemons into the pan together with the eggs.
**2.** Continue to stir over the simmering water until the curd thickens, which will take about 20–25 minutes. Remove from the heat and pour the lemon curd into clean warm jars. Cover and seal while hot, and label when cold.

# Honey and Lemon Curd

*Fills 2 × 8 oz (225 g) jars*

Any honey will do for this recipe, which goes very well with scones and brown bread and butter. Label clearly and cover the tops of the jars with pretty fabric. It will keep for about 6 months in a cool place.

**½ pint (300 ml) honey**
**3 eggs, lightly beaten**
**juice of 2 lemons**
**2 oz (50 g) unsalted butter**

**1.** Place all the ingredients in a double boiler or a mixing bowl placed on top of a saucepan of water. Cook over a low heat, stirring continually, until the mixture thickens enough to coat the back of a wooden spoon.
**2.** Pot into warm clean jars and cover when cold. Will keep for 6 months on a cool larder shelf.

# Mincemeat

*Makes about 5½ lb (2.5 kg)*

Home-made mincemeat is always a very welcome gift. If you are short of time buy a good commercial variety, turn it out into a bowl and stir in a little whisky to taste, which will give the mincemeat a tremendous lift. Stick attractive labels on the jars and cover the tops with circles of fabric.

**1½ lb (675 g) stoned raisins**
**4 oz (100 g) candied peel**
**1 lb (450 g) cooking apples**
**12 oz (350 g) currants    8 oz (225 g) sultanas**
**6 oz (175 g) shredded suet**
**½ level teaspoon mixed spice**
**2 lemons**
**1 lb (450 g) soft brown sugar**
**6 tablespoons rum, brandy or sherry**

**1.** Finely chop or mince the raisins and peel. Peel, core and mince or chop the apples. Place in a large bowl with the other fruit, suet and spice. Grate the rind and squeeze the juice from the lemons, add with the sugar and rum, brandy or sherry to the fruit, and mix very well.
**2.** Cover the bowl with a cloth and leave to stand overnight. Next day turn into clean jars, cover and label.

# Apricot Conserve

*Makes about 5 ½ lb (2.5 kg)*

This recipe does not set as firm as other jams, being more like the Continental jams – perfect with croissants. It makes a very good gift for visitors and I always make a batch each year. Label the jars attractively and cover with a pretty flowered fabric lid.

**1 lb (450 g) dried apricots**
**3 pints (1.5 litres) cold water**
**3 lb (1.4 kg) granulated sugar**
**2 oz (50 g) blanched halved almonds**
**juice of 2 lemons**

**1.** Cut each apricot in quarters and place in a large bowl with the water for 48 hours.
**2.** Turn the fruit and the water into a preserving pan and cook gently until the apricots are soft, about 30–40 minutes. Add the sugar and stir until dissolved. Stir in the almonds and lemon juice and boil rapidly until setting point is reached (when a small amount of jam placed on a cold saucer will form a skin when pushed with the finger). Pot in clean warm jars, cover and label.

# Raspberry Vinegar

*Makes about 1¼ pints (750 ml)*

Use over-ripe or squashy raspberries that perhaps were packed on a wet day. Frozen ones will do well. Use the vinegar in sweet and sour recipes or with hot sponge or syrup puddings. Bottle in attractive small bottles and label. It can be used at once, or will mellow with keeping for a week or two.

**1 pint (600 ml) white vinegar**
**1 lb (450 g) raspberries**
**granulated sugar**

**1.** Place vinegar and raspberries in a bowl and mash the raspberries well to allow the juice to start flowing (a potato masher is very good). Cover with a clean cloth or a piece of cling film, and if using a cloth take care that it does not fall into the vinegar. Leave in a warm place for 3–5 days. Press the fruit again and then strain.
**2.** Measure the juice and add 1 lb (450 g) granulated sugar per pint (600 ml) of raspberry vinegar. Place the vinegar in a saucepan with the sugar and bring slowly to the boil, stirring until dissolved then boil for 10 minutes or until a spoonful placed on a cold saucer is syrupy. Pour into clean small bottles with screw-top lids or corks.

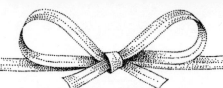

# Clare's Sage Jelly

*Makes about 3 ½ lb (1.5 kg)*

Make this with the last of the windfall apples. It is delicious with pork.

**3 lb (1.4 kg) cooking apples    1 large lemon**
**1½ pint (900 ml) boiling water**
**granulated sugar**
**1 bunch young sage    a little green colouring**

**1.** Wipe the apples, then slice with the lemon, including the peel, core and pips of both. Put in a saucepan with the water, cover and simmer for about 20 minutes or until soft. Mash well and strain through a jelly bag overnight. Measure the juice which will give about 2 pints (a good litre). For each pint (600 ml) allow 1 lb (450 g) sugar.
**2.** Heat the sugar and apple juice in a saucepan until the sugar has dissolved. Very finely chop the smallest tender sage leaves, and then tie the remainder in a bunch and lower into the juice, securing the string to the handle of the pan. Boil rapidly until setting point is reached (when a small amount dropped on a cold saucer forms a skin when pushed with the finger). Remove from the heat.
**3.** Lift out the bunch of sage leaves and discard. Add a few drops of green colouring and stir in the chopped sage. Leave to stand for about 5 minutes before potting so that the jelly will thicken slightly and the sage will be evenly distributed. Pot in small warm jars, cover with a wax disc and screw-top lids.

# Pickled Peaches

These keep very well in the refrigerator for at least 4 days. Make them just before Christmas and then pack into attractive glass jars. They are delicious served with cold ham and turkey.

**1 lb, 14 oz (875 g) can peach halves**
**4 oz (100 g) light soft brown sugar**
**4 tablespoons malt vinegar**
**2 small sticks cinnamon**
**1 rounded teaspoon whole cloves**
**1 rounded teaspoon whole allspice**

**1.** Drain the syrup from the peaches into a saucepan. Add all the other ingredients (except the peaches), bring to the boil and simmer for 5 minutes. Add the peaches, bring back to the boil and simmer for a further 5 minutes. Pour all into a bowl, cover and leave in a cool place overnight.
**2.** Next day pack into jars.

# Spiced Apricots

*Fills about 4 × 8 oz (225 g) jars*

These are lovely with ham, pork, turkey or duck. These are best packed into small glass jars and neatly labelled.

**1 lb (450 g) dried apricots, the kind that require no soaking**
**8 oz (225 g) granulated sugar**
**¼ pint (150 ml) white wine vinegar**
**1 teaspoon whole coriander**
**1 teaspoon whole allspice**
**½ teaspoon whole cloves**

**1.** Place the apricots in a heavy based pan, add the sugar, vinegar and spices, and heat gently until the sugar has dissolved. Bring to the boil and then simmer for 25–30 minutes or until the apricots are tender. Take the apricots from the syrup with a slotted spoon and divide between 4 small warm clean jars.
**2.** Bring the syrup back to the boil and when thick, strain out the spices, and pour syrup over the apricots. Seal the jars while still hot. Best eaten in 2-3 months

# Sweet Mustard Chutney

*Makes about 4 ½ lb (2 kg) chutney*

This is really crisp and goes well with cold meats and cheese.

**1 small marrow, peeled, seeded and finely diced**
**½ cucumber, finely diced**
**2 carrots and 2 onions, grated**
**1 small cauliflower, broken into tiny pieces**
**5 oz (150 g) salt    2½ pints (1.4 litres) water**

SAUCE
**1½ oz (40 g) flour**
**¼ oz (6.2 g)** *each* **of curry powder and turmeric**
**¾ oz (19 g) mustard powder**
**2 pints (a good litre) malt vinegar**
**10 oz (275 g) granulated sugar**

**1.** Place all the prepared vegetables in a large bowl or plastic bucket, add the salt and water, and leave to soak for 24 hours. Next day rinse the vegetables and drain very thoroughly.
**2.** To make the sauce, put the flour and spices in a preserving pan and gradually blend in the vinegar to make a smooth paste. Add the sugar and bring to the boil, stirring until thickened. Add the vegetables, bring back to the boil and boil for 5 minutes. Remove from the heat, pot in clean warm jars, and seal with plastic or vinegar-proof lids.

# Chilli Chutney

*Fills about 5–6 × 1 lb (450 g) jars*

A nice lightly spiced chutney. An ideal way to use up all those small ripe tomatoes that always seem to be in abundance at the end of the season.

**3 lb (1.4 kg) tomatoes**
**2 lb (900 g) onions, chopped**
**1 green pepper, seeded and chopped**
**¾ pint (450 ml) cider vinegar**
**1 tablespoon salt**
**2 teaspoons ground cloves, optional**
**2 teaspoons ground allspice**
**2 teaspoons chilli powder**
**1 teaspoon ground cinnamon**
**8 oz (225 g) light soft brown sugar**

**1.** Place the tomatoes in a bowl, cover with boiling water and leave to stand for 10 seconds. Drain them then peel off the skins, and coarsely chop. Put in a large saucepan with all the ingredients except the sugar and bring to the boil. Simmer for 45 minutes or until the onion is tender.
**2.** Stir in the sugar, bring to the boil and cook for about 30 minutes, stirring occasionally, until a thick chutney consistency. Pour into hot clean jars, cover and label. Store until required.

# Garlic Olives

**1.** There is no real recipe for this. Buy a jar of green olives, stuffed or unstuffed. Drain off the brine, measure the amount and then discard. Rinse the olives in cold water to remove excess salt. Soak the label off the jar and wash and dry thoroughly.

**2.** Return the olives to the jar with 3 cloves of peeled garlic, each one split in three, and a little pickling spice. Pour over a sweet French dressing, using the same amount as the brine. Cover with the lid, label and then store in the refrigerator for up to 2 months.

## SWEET FRENCH DRESSING

**½ clove garlic, crushed**
**½ teaspoon dry mustard**
**½ teaspoon salt**
**a good pinch of freshly ground black pepper**
**1 tablespoon caster sugar**
**¼ pint (150 ml) corn or salad oil**
**4–6 tablespoons cider or white wine vinegar**

Blend the first five ingredients together in a bowl and then gradually mix in the oil with a whisk or spoon. Stir in the vinegar. Taste and adjust seasoning if necessary.

# SWEETS

The type of sweet you are giving determines the packaging. Save old boxes and persuade the children to cover them with brightly coloured paper. Use the base of the box to hold the sweets, and cover the top with cling film, and add a bow of ribbon. Fudge, coconut ice, truffles and stuffed dates are best packed like this and anything at all sticky should be individually wrapped. Coloured paper sweet cases add a touch of distinction. They are easily available from stationery, gift shops and kitchen boutiques.

Fudge and toffee can be packed in the flat foil tins you use in the freezer. For an easy and effective gift, small glass storage jars will hold sugared almonds and show off their delicate colours, but if anything that is liable to turn sticky is to go into a jar make sure that each piece is wrapped in plastic wrapping or Cellophane.

# Scottish Tablet

*Makes 36 squares of tablet*

This is rather like fudge but is harder and has a drier and more granular texture. Pack into any small box or container.

**1 lb (450 g) granulated sugar**
**a scant ½ pint (300 ml) water**
**2 oz (50 g) butter**
**1 small can condensed milk**
**1 teaspoon vanilla essence**

**1.** Grease a 7 inch (17.5 cm) square tin. Place the sugar and water in a heavy based saucepan and heat slowly so that the sugar dissolves and makes a syrup. Add the butter and condensed milk and bring to the boil, stirring carefully. Boil gently and steadily for about 45 minutes, stirring occasionally. Test the tablet by dropping a little into cold water; if it forms a soft ball it is ready.
**2.** Remove the pan from the heat, add the vanilla essence and beat well until the mixture grains and thickens. Pour into the tin. When setting mark into 36 squares with a knife, then leave until quite cold and break into squares.

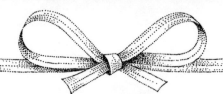

# Fudge

*Makes 36 squares of fudge*

Fudge packs well into any sort of container be it a box attractively covered with paper, or a china mug.

**¼ pint (150 ml) evaporated milk**
**¼ pint (150 ml) water**
**3 oz (75 g) butter**
**1 lb (450 g) granulated sugar**
**about ¼ teaspoon vanilla essence**

**1.** Butter a 7 inch (17.5 cm) square tin. Put the evaporated milk, water, butter and sugar in a heavy saucepan and heat through slowly until the sugar has dissolved, without boiling. Then boil steadily to 237°F (114°C), stirring constantly so that the fudge does not stick. If you do not have a sugar thermometer a small amount of the fudge dropped into a cup of cold water will form a soft ball; if the water becomes cloudy and the fudge dissolves the mixture is not ready.
**2.** Remove the pan from the heat and add the vanilla essence. Cool slightly and then beat until the mixture starts to thicken and crystallise on the spoon. Pour into the tin and leave to set. When firm mark into 36 squares, and store in an airtight tin until required.

## VARIATIONS

*Creamy fudge.* For a more creamy fudge, use ½ pint (300 ml) evaporated milk instead of the evaporated milk and water.

*Chocolate.* Put 1 oz (25 g) cocoa in a saucepan and blend to a smooth paste with the evaporated milk, then add the remaining ingredients (except the vanilla essence) and make as above.

*Raisin or Sultana.* Add about 3 oz (75 g) raisins to the fudge in the saucepan whilst thickening.

*Cherry and Walnut.* Add about 2 oz (50 g) chopped glacé cherries and 2 oz (50 g) roughly chopped walnuts to the fudge in the saucepan whilst thickening.

*Coconut.* Add 2oz (50g) shredded or desiccated coconut to the fudge in the saucepan whilst thickening.

*Ginger.* Add 1 oz (25g) finely chopped stem ginger – take care to well drain the syrup first. Add to the fudge in the saucepan whilst thickening.

*Glacé fruit.* Add 2oz (50g) chopped glacé fruits to the fudge in the saucepan whilst thickening.

# Coconut Ice

*Makes 36 pieces of coconut ice*

A nice creamy recipe and popular with all age groups. You can, if you like, divide the mixture in half and colour one portion pink. Press the pink ice firmly onto the white mixture already in the tin. I like to put these in coloured sweet cases and then place in a transparent box.

**2 egg whites**
**1 lb (450 g) icing sugar, sieved**
**6 oz (175 g) desiccated coconut**
**2 tablespoons water**

**1.** Place the egg whites in a bowl and lightly whisk until frothy. Stir in the sifted icing sugar and then add the coconut and water and mix thoroughly.
**2.** Turn into a lightly greased 7 inch (17.5 cm) square tin and leave in a cool airy place to firm, best left overnight. Cut into 36 squares and if the mixture still seems a little soft it can be left to dry out a little longer.

# Peppermint Creams

*Makes about 20 peppermint creams*

These are very simple and inexpensive to make. They require no cooking and could be made safely by children – with guidance. If you like you can dip one side of the creams into melted plain chocolate. They look very pretty, especially good if packed in a special wine or brandy glass; cover the top with cling film and tie a ribbon around the stem.

**8 oz (225 g) icing sugar**
**1 egg white, lightly beaten**
**a few drops of peppermint essence**

**1.** Sift the icing sugar into a bowl and then stir in sufficient egg white to make a paste. Add a few drops of peppermint essence and knead well. The mixture should be thick and pliable.
**2.** Sieve a little extra icing sugar onto a piece of waxed paper (I save mine from cornflake packets) or non-stick silicone paper. Place the peppermint paste on the paper, cover with another piece, and roll out. Stamp out into rounds of 1 inch (2.5 cm) diameter and about ¼ inch (6 mm) thick. Leave to dry for about 24 hours. Store in an airtight container until required.

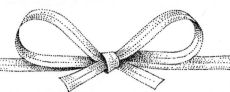

# Chocolate Rum Truffles

*Makes about 50 truffles*

These make marvellous presents. Pack in foil or paper cases, then in small boxes, and keep in the refrigerator.

**6 oz (175 g) plain chocolate**
**2 oz (50 g) butter**
**3 level tablespoons golden syrup**
**4 tablespoons rum**
**4 oz (100 g) ground almonds**
**12 oz (350 g) Madeira cake, crumbled**
**chocolate vermicelli or chocolate powder**
**about 50 small paper sweet cases**

**1.** Break the chocolate into pieces and place with the butter and golden syrup in a bowl and stand over a pan of hot water. Heat gently to melt the chocolate. Remove the bowl from the heat and stir in the rum, ground almonds and cake crumbs and mix well. Chill in the refrigerator until the mixture is firm and easier to handle.
**2.** Spread the vermicelli or chocolate powder into a shallow dish. Take about a rounded teaspoonful of the mixture, shape it into a ball and roll and coat evenly in the vermicelli or chocolate powder. Place in a paper case and leave in the refrigerator until really firm.

# Chocolate Brazils

*Makes about 26 chocolate Brazils*

Always popular, a little chocolate covers quite a lot of nuts. Use plain or milk, whichever you prefer, or coat some nuts in one and some in the other. They are best packed in sweet paper cases and put in a single layer in a box.

**about 3 oz (75 g) chocolate**
**4 oz (100 g) Brazil nuts (about 26 nuts)**

**1.** Break the chocolate into small pieces, place in a bowl and stand over a pan of hot water until melted and smooth. Remove from the heat.
**2.** Spear the nuts with a long fine skewer and then dip into the melted chocolate, turning so that the nut is completely coated. Knock gently on the side of the bowl so that any surplus chocolate drips off. Gently ease the nut from the skewer onto a piece of waxed paper and leave in a cool place to set. Repeat with the remaining nuts and chocolate.

# Buttered Brazils

*Makes about 26 nuts*

As well as buttered brazil nuts you can also make buttered almonds in the same way. When needed, pack the nuts into a small screw-top glass jar and decorate with a bow made of coloured ribbon.

**1 oz (25 g) powdered glucose**
**¼ pint (150 ml) water**
**8 oz (225 g) granulated sugar**
**1 oz (25 g) butter**
**a scant 4 oz (100 g) shelled Brazil nuts**

**1.** Put the glucose, water and sugar in a heavy pan and place on a very low heat until the sugar has completely dissolved. Do not allow to boil. When the sugar has dissolved, boil the syrup to hard crack (310°F or 154°C). If you do not have a sugar thermometer, boil the syrup until golden brown.
**2.** Beat in the butter, then drop in the Brazil nuts, making sure that they are well coated with toffee. Lightly oil a baking sheet and spoon on the nuts individually, and leave to set. Store in an airtight tin until required.

# Peanut Brittle

*Makes 70 pieces of peanut brittle*

This recipe makes up quite a lot of brittle, so will be enough for about three presents. You could of course cut the recipe down and just make a small quantity. Children love to give this to school friends and cousins. Pack in small bags and tie with a pretty ribbon.

**12 oz (350 g) unsalted peanuts, skinned**
**14 oz (400 g) granulated sugar**
**6 oz (175 g) light soft brown sugar**
**6 oz (175 g) golden syrup    ¼ pint (150 ml) water**
**2 oz (50 g) butter**
**¼ level teaspoon bicarbonate of soda**

**1.** Grease a shallow tin 13 × 9 inches (32.5 × 22.5 cm), and put the nuts (on a separate tray or tin) in the oven at the lowest setting until just warm. Put the sugars, syrup and water in a large heavy based saucepan, and heat gently, stirring all the time, until the sugar has dissolved. Stir in the butter, then bring to the boil. Boil rapidly without stirring until temperature just reaches the hard crack stage (300°F or 149°C). Remove the pan from the heat, stir in the bicarbonate of soda and nuts, mix well and then turn straight into the greased tin.
**2.** Leave to cool and then mark into squares. When almost set break into pieces, and store in an airtight tin until required.

# Fruit and Nut Clusters

*Makes about 20 clusters*

Very easy to make, fruit and nut clusters are always popular with young and old alike. No need to use just peanuts, but try almonds or walnuts for a change, roughly chopped. If made in paper sweet cases these look nice in a flat box, otherwise pack in a glass jar.

**4 oz (100 g) plain or milk chocolate**
**(use cooking chocolate or chocolate chips)**
**1 tablespoon golden syrup**
**2 teaspoons water**
**3 oz (75 g) raisins**
**1 oz (25 g) glacé cherries, chopped**
**2 oz (50 g) salted peanuts**

**1.** Place the chocolate broken into small pieces in a basin with the golden syrup and water and stand over a pan of hot water until melted and smooth.
**2.** Remove the pan from the heat and stir in the fruit and nuts and mix thoroughly. Place the mixture in small spoonfuls in sweet cases or on greaseproof paper until set.

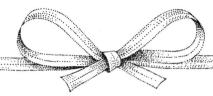

# Marron Glacé

*Makes about 1 lb (450 g)*

If you are going to store these sweets for long they are best wrapped in foil. Pack in an attractive container, cover and label.

**8 oz (225 g) dried chestnuts    4 oz (100 g) granulated sugar**
**4 oz (100 g) powdered glucose    1 teaspoon vanilla essence**

**1.** Place the chestnuts in a bowl, cover with cold water and leave to soak overnight. Next day drain, place in a saucepan and cover with fresh water. Bring slowly to the boil and cook until tender (about 30–45 minutes). Drain carefully in a sieve so that they do not break.
**2.** Place the sugar and glucose in a small saucepan, add ½ pint (300 ml) water and stir over a low heat until the sugar has dissolved. Bring to the boil, add the chestnuts and bring back to the boil. Remove from the heat, cover and leave in a warm place for 24 hours. Remove the pan lid, bring chestnuts to the boil slowly, then cover the pan, remove from the heat and leave for another 24 hours. Add the vanilla essence, stir gently, bring to the boil slowly, cover and leave overnight as before.
**3.** Carefully lift the chestnuts out of the syrup onto a wire rack over a plate. Leave to drain. Store in a cardboard or wooden box, lined with waxed paper and with waxed paper between the layers or wrap each one in foil.

# Stuffed Dates

I always seem to have a little spare marzipan after covering the Christmas cake and this is the perfect way to use it up. A small amount of marzipan fills quite a lot of dates. I like to put them in sweet cases and arrange in a single layer in a box. They are very pretty when filled with different colour marzipan and decorated with flaked almonds.

**almond paste or marzipan**
**food colouring**
**dates**
**a little sugar**
**almond flakes**

**1.** Take the almond paste or marzipan and divide in half. Leave one piece as it is but colour the other with a little food colouring (green looks good).
**2.** Make a small slit in each date along the side, remove the stone and then fill the cavity with a small piece of almond paste. Roll the stuffed date in sugar and then decorate with a flaked almond. Place in sweet cases and store in a tin until required.

# CAKES

Those cakes that keep well make the most convenient presents, unless the recipient has been warned in advance of what is to come and you know that the cake will be eaten at once. It is usually a wise precaution, in any case, to announce that a special occasion cake is being made – for birthday, Christmas, Easter or whatever – and so avoid the danger of anyone having too much of a good thing.

Cakes that can be stored in the freezer may be given in their foil or plastic freezer containers, clearly labelled. Otherwise, use the bottom halves of cardboard boxes, for packing and cover with coloured paper and ribbon.

Cakes need not be elaborate. Often a plain madeira, or even a currant loaf, will be more welcome than the richest fruit cake.

# Almond Slices

*Makes 12 slices*

Really almondy. Make in a new tin and give with the cake, or cut into slices and pack attractively in a box.

**6 oz (175 g) plain flour**
**1½ oz (40 g) hard margarine    1½ oz (40 g) lard**
**about 2 tablespoons cold water**

**FILLING**
**4 oz (100 g) butter    4 oz (100 g) caster sugar**
**1 egg, beaten    4 oz (100 g) ground rice**
**½ teaspoon almond essence**
**2 tablespoons raspberry jam    flaked almonds**

**1.** Heat the oven to 400°F, 200°C, gas mark 6. To make the pastry, place the flour in a bowl, and rub in the margarine and lard cut in small pieces. Add sufficient cold water and mix to a firm dough. Roll out the pastry and line a tin 11 x 7 inches (27.5 x 17.5 cm). Prick the base with a fork. Chill whilst making the filling.
**2.** Melt the butter in a saucepan, stir in the sugar, cook for a minute, then mix in the egg, ground rice and almond essence.
**3.** Spread the jam over the pastry and then pour over the filling. Sprinkle with almonds and bake in the oven for 30 minutes until risen and golden brown. Leave to cool in the tin and then mark into slices.

# Mincemeat and Almond Slices

*Makes 16 mincemeat and almond slices*

These have a crumbly pastry that is difficult to handle, but it makes delicious cakes. They freeze well wrapped in foil or will keep well in the refrigerator. Pack in a box or tin with an airtight lid.

**8 oz (225 g) self-raising flour**
**3 oz (75 g) soft brown sugar    2 oz (50 g) ground almonds**
**6 oz (175 g) butter**
**1 large egg    1 teaspoon lemon juice**
**14½ oz (411 g) jar of mincemeat**
**1 oz (25 g) flaked almonds**

**1.** Place the flour, sugar and almonds in a large roomy bowl, add the butter cut in small pieces and rub in. Beat the egg and lemon juice together and then add all but a teaspoonful to the dry ingredients and mix well. Divide the dough in half and refrigerate for an hour.
**2.** Heat the oven to 350°F, 180°C, gas mark 4. Roll out one half of the dough thinly and use to line a Swiss roll tin 13 x 9 inches (32.5 x 22.5 cm). If the dough splits do not worry, just patch together. Spread the mincemeat over. Roll out the remaining dough and lay on top of the mincemeat, lightly brush with the last of the beaten egg and sprinkle all over with flaked almonds. Mark into 16 squares and then bake in the oven for about 30 minutes until golden brown. Leave to cool in the tin and then cut into the marked squares.

# Lemon Baklava

*Serves 8*

Phyllo pastry can be bought in delicatessen and Greek shops. This is really best given in the tin in which it was cooked, covered with cling film.

**8 oz (225 g) phyllo pastry    4 oz (100 g) unsalted butter, melted**
**4 oz (100 g) walnuts, chopped finely    1 oz (25 g) caster sugar**

**LEMON SYRUP**
**¼ pint (150 ml) water    12 oz (350 g) caster sugar**
**thinly peeled rind and juice of 2 lemons**

**1.** Heat the oven to 400°F, 200°C, gas mark 6. Butter a Swiss roll tin 11 × 7 inches (27.5 × 17.5 cm). Cut the phyllo pastry in half so that it is roughly the size of the tin. Lay 1 sheet of pastry in the tin, brush with butter and continue until there are 8 layers in the tin. Brush the top layer with butter and sprinkle with nuts and sugar. Top with a further 8 layers of pastry, brushing with butter as before. Brush the top with more butter and cut through to the tin in diamond shapes.
**2.** Bake for about 25-30 minutes until pale golden brown. Cool.
**3.** Put the water into a pan, add the sugar and thinly peeled lemon rind, and bring to the boil slowly. Simmer 15 minutes without a lid, then remove from heat and add lemon juice. Pour over the cold baklava or cool the syrup and pour over a hot baklava. Serve with whipped cream.

# Iced American Brownies

*Makes 16 brownies*

This can be made in a 9 inch (22.5 cm) square foil container and then iced in the container when cool.

**2 eggs    8 oz (225 g) caster sugar**
**3 tablespoons cocoa**
**3 oz (75 g) soft margarine    2 oz (50 g) self-raising flour**
**4 oz (100 g) sultanas**
**4 oz (100 g) chopped nuts (walnuts, hazelnuts or almonds)**

**FUDGE ICING**
**1½ oz (40 g) butter    1 oz (25 g) cocoa, sieved**
**2 tablespoons milk    4 oz (100 g) icing sugar, sieved**

**1.** Heat the oven to 350°F, 180°C, gas mark 4. Place all the ingredients for the brownies in a large bowl, beat well and then turn into the foil container. Smooth the top and bake for about 30–40 minutes, until the mixture has shrunk from the sides and is firm to the touch. Leave to cool.
**2.** To make the icing, melt the butter in a small saucepan, stir in the cocoa and cook gently for 1 minute. Remove from the heat, add the milk and icing sugar, and beat well until smooth. Cool, stirring occasionally, until thick enough to spread over the brownie. Leave to cool, and mark into 16 squares.

# Queenswood Gingerbread

*Makes 32 pieces*

This recipe was discovered at the back of a desk on a carol service sheet for Queenswood school, dated 1946. It seemed well worth trying and I found it moist and full of flavour. Wrap in cling film and label neatly.

**8 oz (225 g) plain flour**
**1 level teaspoon baking powder**
**1 teaspoon mixed spice    1 teaspoon ground ginger**
**5 oz (150 g) golden syrup    5 oz (150 g) black treacle**
**4 oz (100 g) dark soft brown sugar**
**4 oz (100 g) lard**
**2 eggs    2 tablespoons milk**

**1.** Heat the oven to 325°F, 160°C, gas mark 3. Grease and line with greased greaseproof paper an 8 inch (20 cm) square tin. Put the flour, baking powder, spice and ginger in a bowl and make a well in the centre. Place the syrup, treacle, sugar and lard in a saucepan and heat through gently until the lard has melted and the sugar dissolved. Remove from the heat and stir into the flour with the eggs and milk and beat thoroughly.
**2.** Pour into the tin and then bake in the oven for about 45 minutes or until the gingerbread is firm to the touch and has shrunk slightly from the sides of the tin. Leave to cool in the tin, then remove, peel off the paper and store in an airtight tin for at least 3 or 4 days before cutting.

# Welsh Currant Bread

*Makes a 2 lb (900 g) loaf*

This keeps remarkably well. Soak the fruit overnight in cider instead of hot tea if you like. Wrap in cling film for presentation.

**6 oz (175 g) currants**
**6 oz (175 g) sultanas**
**8 oz (225 g) muscovado sugar**
**½ pint (300 ml) hot tea**
**10 oz (275 g) self-raising flour**
**1 egg, beaten**

**1.** Put the fruit and sugar in a bowl, pour over the hot tea, stir well, cover and leave to stand overnight.
**2.** Grease and line with greased greaseproof paper a 2 lb (900 g) loaf tin. Heat the oven to 300°F, 150°C, gas mark 2. Stir the flour and egg into the fruit, mix thoroughly and turn into the tin. Bake in the oven for about 1¾ hours or until it has shrunk away from the sides of the tin. Turn out onto a wire rack and leave to cool. Serve sliced with butter or just as it is.

# Cherry and Pineapple Loaf

*Makes a 2 lb (900 g) loaf*

This is a very moist cake that keeps well in an airtight tin. Dry the cherries thoroughly so that all moisture is removed, then they don't sink! Wrap in cling film and label neatly.

**3 oz (75 g) glacé cherries   4 oz (100 g) glacé pineapple**
**8 oz (225 g) self-raising flour**
**6 oz (175 g) soft margarine**
**6 oz (175 g) caster sugar   3 large eggs**
**finely grated rind of 1 lemon**
**2 oz (50 g) ground almonds**

**1.** Heat the oven to 350°F, 180°C, gas mark 4, and grease and line with greased greaseproof paper a 2 lb (900 g) loaf tin. Cut each cherry in quarters, put in a sieve and rinse under running water. Drain well and dry thoroughly on kitchen paper. Quarter the glacé pineapple. Place all the remaining ingredients in a large bowl and beat well for one minute and then lightly fold in the glacé cherries and pineapple. The mixture will be fairly stiff.
**2.** Turn into the tin and bake in the oven for about 1¼ hours or until a warm skewer inserted in the centre comes out clean. If the cake looks to be getting too brown, cover with a piece of foil. Leave to cool in the tin for 10 minutes then turn out and finish cooling on a wire rack. Store in an airtight tin.

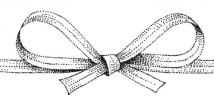

# Orange and Lemon Sandwich

*Makes a 7 inch (17.5 cm) cake*

Although good cooks have no problem in quickly making a Victoria sandwich, non-cooks find it a great luxury, and will be delighted with one as a gift. Place on a cake board and lightly cover with cling film or foil.

**4 oz (100 g) soft margarine**
**4 oz (100 g) caster sugar**
**finely grated rind of 1 orange**
**finely grated rind of ½ lemon**
**2 large eggs, beaten**
**4 oz (100 g) self-raising flour**
**4 tablespoons lemon curd**

**1.** Heat the oven to 350°F, 180°C, gas mark 4. Grease and line with greased greaseproof paper 2 × 7 inch (17.5 cm) straight sided sandwich tins. Cream the margarine, sugar, orange and lemon rind until light and fluffy. Add the eggs a little at a time, beating well after each addition. Sieve the flour and add a spoonful with the last amount of egg to prevent it curdling. Fold in the remaining flour with a metal spoon to make a soft dropping consistency. Divide the mixture equally between the tins.
**2.** Bake in the oven for 25–30 minutes until pale gold and the centre of the sponge springs back into place when lightly pressed with the finger. Turn the sponges onto a wire rack to cool, and remove the paper. When quite cold sandwich together with lemon curd and, if liked, sprinkle with a little caster sugar.

# Wheatmeal Fruit Cake

*Makes a 7 inch (17.5cm) cake*

A moist everyday fruit cake, the wheatmeal flour gives a crunchy texture. Wrap in foil or cling film.

2 oz (50 g) glacé cherries
2 oz (50 g) walnuts, chopped
5 oz (150 g) soft margarine
5 oz (150 g) muscovado sugar
2 eggs    8 tablespoons milk
8 oz (225 g) wheatmeal flour
2 level teaspoons baking powder
5 oz (150 g) sultanas
5 oz (150 g) raisins

**1.** Heat the oven to 300°F, 150°C, gas mark 2. Line a 7 inch (17.5 cm) round cake tin with greased greaseproof paper. Place all the ingredients in a large bowl and beat well until the mixture is thoroughly blended, about 2–3 minutes.
**2.** Place in the tin, smooth the top and bake in the oven for about $2^{1}/_{4}$ hours. The cake is cooked if it has shrunk slightly from the sides of the tin and a warm skewer inserted in the centre comes out clean. Leave to cool in the tin, then remove the paper and store in an airtight tin until required.

# Swiss Chocolate Cake

*Serves 8–10*

A very special cake that should be made, delivered and eaten all on the same day. Place on a board and transport carefully!

**6 large eggs, size 2, separated**
**5 oz (150 g) caster sugar    2 oz (50 g) cocoa, sieved**
**15 oz (425 g) can stoneless black cherries in a heavy syrup**
**3 tablespoons sherry**
**½ pint (300 ml) double cream, lightly whipped**
**chocolate flake**

**1.** Heat the oven to 350ºF, 180ºC, gas mark 4. Grease and line with greased greaseproof paper 2 × 8 inch (20 cm) sandwich tins. Place the yolks in a bowl with the caster sugar and cocoa and whisk until thick. Whisk the egg whites in a large bowl until the mixture will form stiff peaks, then add 1 tablespoon of the yolk mixture, and fold in the remainder. Turn into the tins and bake for 20 minutes. Remove from the oven, cool in the tins for 5 minutes, then turn out, peel off the paper and leave to cool on a wire rack.

**2.** Drain the cherries, and mix 2 tablespoons of the juice with the sherry. Place 1 cake on a board and sprinkle over the sherry mixture. Cover with half the cream and cherries, reserving 8 for decoration. Cover with the remaining cake and spread with cream. Arrange the 8 cherries on top and keep in a cool place until ready to serve. Sprinkle with lightly crushed chocolate flake.

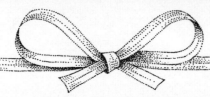

# Chocolate Marble Cake

*Serves about 16*

An attractive cake. Pack in a single layer in a box or tin.

**6 oz (175 g) self-raising flour   2 level teaspoons baking powder**
**6 oz (175 g) caster sugar**
**6 oz (175 g) soft margarine   3 eggs**
**1 level tablespoon cocoa powder   1 tablespoon hot water**

**ICING**
**4 oz (100 g) plain chocolate   3 oz (75 g) butter**
**4 oz (100 g) sieved icing sugar**

**1.** Heat the oven to 375°F, 190°C, gas mark 5. Grease and line with greased greaseproof paper a tin 11 × 7 × 1½ inches (27.5 × 17.5 × 4 cm). Put the flour, baking powder, sugar, margarine and eggs in a large bowl and beat until smooth. Dot half the mixture in teaspoonfuls over the base of the cake tin. Blend the cocoa and water together and stir into the remaining mixture, dot between the plain mixture, and swirl a little with a knife. Bake for about 30 minutes. Remove and cool in the tin for about 5 minutes, then remove the paper and leave to cool on a wire rack.
**2.** Break chocolate into small pieces and place in saucepan with butter. Heat until mixture has melted. Remove from heat and beat for 2 minutes until smooth. Beat in icing sugar, then knead to a smooth dough. Smooth onto cake. Leave to set, then cut into about 16 slices.

# Old–fashioned Madeira Cake

*Makes an 8 inch (20 cm) cake*

A few years ago we won a holiday in Madeira. I have wonderful memories of eating real moist Madeira cake at 11 a.m. with a glass of Madeira – in glorious sunshine. This recipe is particularly good and very simple.

**6 oz (175 g) soft butter    6 oz (175 g) caster sugar
3 eggs    8 oz (225 g) self-raising flour, sieved
grated rind and juice of 1 small orange
grated rind of 1 small lemon
1 level tablespoon honey    1 thin slice candied citrus peel (optional)**

**1.** Heat the oven to 325°F, 160°C, gas mark 3. Grease an 8 inch (20 cm) loose-bottomed cake tin. Cream the butter and sugar until light and fluffy. Add the eggs one at a time, beating well between each addition, adding 2 tablespoons of flour with the last egg. Fold in remaining flour, rind, juice and honey. Turn into the greased tin, and place the peel carefully on top.
**2.** Bake for about 1¼ hours until evenly risen, very pale brown, and a fine skewer comes out clean. Leave to cool in the tin for 10 minutes, then turn out onto a wire rack.

# Traditional Fruit Cake

*Makes an 8 inch (20 cm) cake*

This is a very moist and rich cake topped with glacé fruits. It can also be transformed into a Christmas cake by omitting the topping here, and covering with almond paste and icing, see following recipes.

**1 lb (450 g) mixed dried fruit   8 stoned prunes, chopped**
**4 tablespoons sherry**
**grated rind and juice of 1 orange**
**2 oz (50 g) glacé cherries, quartered   2 oz (50 g) walnuts, chopped**
**6 oz (175 g) soft butter**
**5 oz (150 g) dark soft brown sugar**
**7 oz (200 g) plain flour   2 level teaspoons mixed spice**
**4 eggs, lightly beaten**
**2 level tablespoons each apricot jam and black treacle**

**TOPPING**
**apricot jam   glacé cherries   glacé fruits   mixed nuts**

**1.** Grease and line an 8 inch (20 cm) round cake tin with greased greaseproof paper. The night before, measure the dried fruit and prunes into a saucepan and pour over the sherry and the orange rind and juice. Heat over a moderate heat, stirring for about 5 minutes. Cover and leave in a warm place overnight, by then the liquid will be mostly absorbed. Next day add the cherries and nuts.

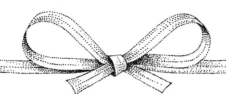

**2.** Cream the butter and sugar until light and fluffy. Sieve the flour and the spice together, then add half the flour to the butter/sugar mixture. Blend in, then add the eggs little by little, beating well. Beat in the jam and treacle, then fold in the remaining flour and fruit.

**3.** Turn into the tin, smooth the top and bake in the oven for about 2¼ hours at 275°F, 140°C, gas mark 1. Test with a warm skewer; if it comes out clean, the cake is done. The top will be golden brown. Leave to cool in the tin, then brush the top with apricot jam and arrange the cherries, glacé fruits and nuts on top and brush again with jam. Store in a tin for up to 3 weeks.

## ROYAL ICING

*Covers an 8 inch (20 cm) round cake*

**1½ lb (675 g) icing sugar**
**4 egg whites    3 teaspoons lemon juice**
**1½ teaspoons glycerine**

Sieve the icing sugar. Whisk the egg whites in a bowl until they become frothy. Add the icing sugar a spoonful at a time. Then add the lemon juice and glycerine. Beat the icing until it is very stiff and white and will stand up in peaks. Put the icing around the sides and over the top of the cake and rough up so that it forms soft peaks. Leave to become firm in a cool place.

# Almond Paste

*Covers an 8 inch (20 cm) round cake*

**6 oz (175 g) ground almonds
6 oz (175 g) icing sugar, sifted
6 oz (175 g) caster sugar
3 egg yolks, lightly beaten
almond essence   juice of ½ lemon
melted apricot jam**

**1.** Mix together the icing sugar, ground almonds and sugar. Add the egg yolks. Flavour first with essence, then with lemon juice. Work into a smooth ball – do not over-knead. Divide into 2 pieces, two-thirds to one-third.

**2.** Cut out a circle of greaseproof paper to fit the top of the cake, and a strip to fit around the side. Sugar them with a little caster sugar. Roll out the smaller piece of paste to fit the circle and the larger piece to fit the strip generously. For the sides it helps to roll a long sausage shape of almond paste and then to flatten it. Brush the top of the cake with apricot jam, then put the paste in position, leaving the paper on the top. Turn the cake over.

**3.** Brush the side of the cake with melted apricot jam, then fix on the strip of paste and remove the paper. Neaten the edges with a palette knife and roll a straight sided tin around the cake to smooth. Turn the cake upright and put on a board. Level the top with a rolling pin. Cover and leave in a cool place for 5–6 days to dry.

# BISCUITS

These should always be packed and presented in airtight containers. Tins with well fitting lids or plastic freezer boxes are ideal and there is no reason why you should not make them look pretty. Cover a tin with plain coloured paper, for instance, and stick an attractive label on top. Or cut out a piece of decorative wallpaper to fit the top of a plastic box. Fasten it to the lid with a bow of matching ribbon.

If you are feeling extravagant, a specially bought decorative biscuit tin can be part of the present.

Small biscuits look well packed in transparent glass storage jars. There are plenty of interesting shaped jars to choose from.

Don't forget savoury biscuits. They are certain favourites, particularly with men, and excellent to serve with drinks.

# A Really Good Shortbread

*Makes 16 pieces of shortbread*

The best recipe for shortbread that I know. Pack in an attractive box, cover and decorate with a ribbon.

**6 oz (175 g) plain flour**
**1½ oz (40 g) cornflour**
**1½ oz (40 g) semolina**
**6 oz (175 g) butter**
**3 oz (75 g) caster sugar**

**1.** Heat the oven to 325°F, 160°C, gas mark 3. Sift the flour, cornflour and semolina into a bowl. In another bowl cream the butter until soft, then add the sugar and beat until light and fluffy. Work in the flours and then knead well together.

**2.** Press out the shortbread into a shallow greased tin 11 × 7 inches (27.5 × 17.5 cm), flattening the dough with the knuckles. Prick well with a fork, mark into 16 fingers with the back of a knife. Bake in the oven for about 35 minutes or until a very pale golden brown. Leave to cool in the tin for 15 minutes then cut through where the shortbread is marked and then carefully lift onto a wire rack to finish cooking. Store in an airtight tin until required.

# Easter Biscuits

*Makes 24 biscuits*

Good at any time of year. Pack in a plastic bag or box.

**5 oz (150 g) butter**
**4 oz (100 g) caster sugar**
**finely grated rind of 1 lemon**
**2 egg yolks**
**8 oz (225 g) plain flour**
**2 oz (50 g) currants**
**a little egg white**

**1.** Cream the butter with the sugar and lemon rind until light and fluffy. Beat in the egg yolks and then stir in the sifted flour and currants. Knead lightly until smooth and then leave in the refrigerator or a cool place for an hour. Heat the oven to 350°F, 180°C, gas mark 4, and lightly grease 2 large baking sheets.
**2.** Turn the dough onto a lightly floured table, roll out to an ⅛ inch (3 mm) thickness, and cut into rounds with a 3 inch (7.5 cm) fluted cutter. Brush with a little lightly beaten egg white, dredge with caster sugar and place on the baking sheets. Bake for about 12–15 minutes until a pale golden brown. Transfer to a wire rack, leave to cool, then store in an airtight tin until required.

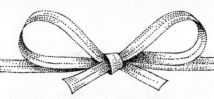

# Danish Butter Biscuits

*Makes about 36 biscuits*

It is important to use butter in these biscuits as the flavour really does come through. They look lovely if packed in a glass storage jar and tied with a ribbon.

**8 oz (225 g) unsalted butter, softened**
**4 oz (100 g) caster sugar**
**1 egg yolk**
**4 oz (100 g) plain flour**
**4 oz (100 g) self-raising flour**
**3 oz (75 g) ground almonds**

**1.** Heat the oven to 375°F, 190°C, gas mark 5. Lightly grease 3 or 4 baking trays. Cream the butter and sugar together until blended and then beat in the egg yolk. Add the remaining ingredients and mix well.
**2.** Place in a large piping bag fitted with a large rose pipe and pipe the mixture into rounds on the trays. Bake in the oven for about 10–12 minutes until a pale honey colour. Leave to cool on the trays for a minute then transfer to a cooling rack and if liked dust with a little icing sugar. Store in an airtight tin until required.

# Botermopen

*Makes about 64 biscuits*

Pack these Dutch biscuits in a plastic bag tied with a pretty ribbon or in any large necked jar or container.

**12 oz (350 g) unsalted butter    finely grated rind of 1 lemon**
**8 oz (225 g) caster sugar    1 lb (450 g) plain flour**
**2 oz (50 g) granulated sugar**

**1.** Heat the oven to 325°F, 160°C, gas mark 3. Lightly grease 4 large baking trays. Cream the butter and rind until soft. Beat in the caster sugar until light, then blend in the flour and mix until smooth. Using your hands, work the mixture together and divide into 4 equal portions. Roll out to form 4 × 6 inch (15 cm) sausages and roll them in the granulated sugar. Wrap in foil and chill until firm.
**2.** Cut each sausage into about 16 slices and place, apart, on baking trays. Bake for about 25 minutes or until pale golden brown at the edges. Cool on a wire rack.

# Nutty Biscuits

*Makes 16 nutty biscuits*

These biscuits would, I am sure, be welcomed by a whole-food addict. They are wonderfully crunchy and full of goodness. Pack in a plastic bag, tied with ribbon, or fill a glass storage jar.

**4 oz (100 g) butter, softened**
**2 oz (50 g) light soft brown sugar or demerara**
**2 oz (50 g) chopped mixed nuts**
**4 oz (100 g) wholemeal flour**
**4 teaspoons milk**
**16 walnut quarters or 16 almond halves**

**1.** Heat the oven to 375°F, 190°C, gas mark 5, and grease 2 baking sheets. Cream the butter and sugar together until soft, then beat in the nuts, work in the flour and milk, and mix thoroughly.
**2.** Divide the mixture into 16 pieces, and roll into small balls. Place on the baking sheets, flatten slightly and place a nut in the centre of each. Bake in the oven for 15–20 minutes until golden brown. Lift off and leave to cool on a wire rack.

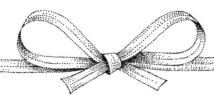

# Grandfather's Gingernuts

*Makes about 50 gingernuts*

The older generation love old-fashioned biscuits like these, which are lovely and inexpensive to make. Place in a plastic bag and tie with a ribbon or pack into a glass cookie jar.

**12 oz (350 g) self-raising flour**
**4 oz (100 g) demerara sugar**
**4 oz (100 g) soft brown sugar**
**1 teaspoon bicarbonate of soda**
**3 good teaspoons ground ginger**
**1 egg**
**4 oz (100 g) butter**
**1 generous tablespoon golden syrup**

**1.** Heat the oven to 325°F, 160°C, gas mark 3. Grease several baking sheets. Mix all the dry ingredients together, then add the beaten egg, and the butter and syrup which have been melted together. Mix thoroughly.
**2.** Roll into small balls and place on a greased baking tray about 2 inches (5 cm) apart. Bake in the oven for 20 minutes, when they will look like bought gingernut cookies. Lift off the baking sheet and cool on a wire rack. Store in an airtight tin until required.

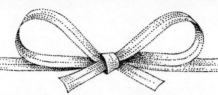

# Coconut Bars

*Makes 18 coconut bars*

Very crunchy and 'more-ish'. I like to put these in a plastic bag and tie them up with a ribbon for presentation.

**5 oz (150 g) soft margarine**
**5 oz (150 g) demerara sugar**
**5 oz (150 g) quick porridge oats**
**1 oz (25 g) desiccated coconut**

**1.** Heat the oven to 325°F, 160°C, gas mark 3. Grease a shallow tin 11 × 7 inches (27.5 × 17.5 cm). Cream the margarine and sugar together until well blended and then stir in the oats and coconut and mix thoroughly.
**2.** Press into the tin and bake for 40–45 minutes until golden brown. Remove from the oven and leave for 10 minutes, then mark into 18 squares and leave to become quite cold in the tin. Lift out of the tin and store in an airtight container.

# Florentines

*Makes about 36 florentines*

Really crisp and delicious, they take time to make, but are lovely to serve with ice creams and mousses, or as biscuits at a coffee morning. They're very brittle, so pack carefully in a firm container and cover with cling film. There is *meant* to be no flour in the recipe, and they are quite tricky to make. If liked, a little melted chocolate may be spread on the flat side once coated then a zig zag effect made with a fork.

**4 oz (100 g) caster sugar   4 oz (100 g) butter
4 oz (100 g) shredded almonds
2 oz (50 g) small sultanas   2 oz (50 g) glacé cherries, chopped**

**1.** Heat the oven to 350°F, 180°C, gas mark 4, and line 4 baking trays with non-stick vegetable parchment. Place the sugar and butter in a heavy saucepan and heat gently, stirring until the sugar has dissolved and boiling point is reached. Remove from the heat and stir in the remaining ingredients.

**2.** Place some of the mixture in small teaspoonfuls well spaced on the baking trays. Bake for about 10 minutes until a golden brown. Remove and leave to cool on the trays for about 5 minutes, then carefully lift off and place on a wire rack. Bake the rest of the mixture in the same way – the parchment can be re-used. Keep in an airtight container or freeze in a plastic box.

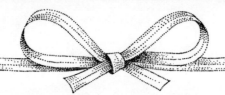

# Savoury Cheese Biscuits

*Makes about 20 cheese biscuits*

These are ideal to give with some Potted Stilton or Fresh Herb Cheese. Pack carefully in a box as they are crisp.

**4 oz (100 g) soft margarine**
**2 oz (50 g) ground rice**
**2 oz (50 g) self-raising flour**
**2 oz (50 g) wholemeal flour**
**3 oz (75 g) grated mature Cheddar cheese**
**½ teaspoon salt**
**½ teaspoon mustard powder**
**a good pinch cayenne pepper**

**1.** Put all the ingredients in a bowl and work together until well blended, using a wooden spoon. Turn onto a floured surface, knead well and then shape into a roll about 6 inches (15 cm) long. Chill for an hour.
**2.** Heat the oven to 350°F, 180°C, gas mark 4, and grease 2 baking sheets. Cut the roll into thin slices, place on a baking sheet, and sprinkle with some extra wholemeal flour. Bake in the oven for about 15–20 minutes until a pale golden brown. Leave to cool on a wire rack, then store in an airtight tin.

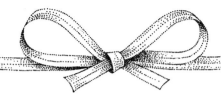

# Cheese Straws

An ideal present to give to men. Pack carefully in a box or tin and cover.

**8 oz (225 g) plain flour
salt and pepper
4 oz (100 g) butter
4 oz (100 g) full flavoured Cheddar cheese, grated
a little beaten egg**

**1.** Heat the oven to 400°F, 200°C, gas mark 6, and lightly grease some baking sheets. Put the flour in a bowl with the salt and pepper, add the butter cut in small pieces and rub in with the fingertips until the mixture resembles fine breadcrumbs. Stir in the cheese, then add sufficient beaten egg to make a firm dough. Turn out onto a floured surface and knead lightly until smooth.

**2.** Roll out to approximately ¼ inch (6 mm) thickness and cut the dough into narrow strips, rings, circles or any fancy shape required. Place on the baking sheets and bake for about 8–10 minutes or until a pale golden brown. Leave to cool on the baking sheets for a minute or two and then lift onto a wire rack to finish cooling. Store in an airtight tin until required.

# PÂTÉS & TERRINES

Give these as soon after making as you can and they will be received in top condition. Potted foods freeze most successfully but ideally they should not be kept in the freezer for more than three months. Label them accordingly.

Pack them in small pots or jars, in foil containers or small plastic cups – unless you want to make a small china terrine part of the present.

There is no need to give large amounts. A small jar of smoked salmon pâté, made for economy from scraps and awkwardly shaped pieces, is a sure-fire treat. Or use smoked mackerel or kipper fillets to make a less expensive variety. Dips to take to parties will naturally be in bigger quantities and are best carried in large foil dishes.

Potted cheeses of two or three different kinds can be packed in identical small jars and presented together in a box. A liver pâté liberally laced with brandy makes a very special present.

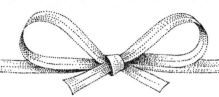

# Avocado Pâté Dip

*Serves 8-12*

This really has to be made, given and eaten on the same day. Nice to take to a party when you have been asked to give a dip. Pack into a small foil or plastic container that can be left at the party; there is nothing worse than asking for a dish back as you go out of the front door!

**1 level teaspoon salt**
**freshly ground black pepper**
**1 level teaspoon made mustard**
**2 level teaspoons caster sugar**
**6 tablespoons salad oil**
**juice of ½ lemon**
**2 ripe avocado pears**
**2 tomatoes, skinned and seeded and chopped**
**1 tablespoon chopped chives**

**1.** Put the salt, pepper, mustard and sugar into a small bowl. Blend in the oil a little at a time, then blend in the lemon juice.
**2.** Cut the pears in half, remove the stones and scoop the flesh out into another bowl. Mash with a fork until quite smooth. Gradually beat in the dressing and then fold in the tomatoes and chives. Turn into a small dish and serve with pieces of crisp raw vegetables.

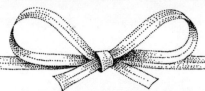

# Taramasalata

*Serves 4*

A quick Greek pâté, present it in one of those small bought pâté dishes. Make a nice label saying serve with hot toast and butter or with pitta bread.

**8 oz (225 g) smoked cod's roe (may be bought in a jar)**
**2 small slices white bread with crusts removed**
**2 tablespoons milk**
**1 clove garlic, crushed (optional)**
**¼ pint (150 ml) less 2 tablespoons oil**
**2 tablespoons lemon juice**
**salt and pepper**
**2 bay leaves to garnish**

**1.** Remove and discard the skin from the cod's roe, then reduce the roe to a paste in a blender or processor. Soak the bread in the milk, then squeeze out as much milk as possible. Add the bread to the roe and blend or mash again with the garlic if used. Add the oil 1 teaspoon at a time until all has been absorbed. Stir in the lemon juice and seasoning.
**2.** Turn into a small dish and chill well. When ready to serve, garnish the dish with bay leaves. Serve with hot buttered toast.

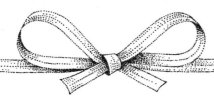

# Smoked Salmon Pâté

*Serves 4*

Use smoked salmon pieces for this recipe – it is the ideal way to use up the ends of a side – and pieces can be bought reasonably cheaply from your fishmonger. This is a special recipe to give a friend or relation. Make it in a pretty small china dish or pot that can be part of the present.

**4 oz (100 g) smoked salmon pieces**
**2 oz (50 g) cream cheese**
**2 oz (50 g) butter, melted**
**1 tablespoon lemon juice**
**freshly ground black pepper**
**a little salt**

**1.** Put the salmon, cream cheese, half the butter, lemon juice, pepper and salt in a blender or processor and purée until smooth.
**2.** Turn into a small pot or dish (½ pint or 300 ml size) and smooth the top. Pour over the remaining melted butter and leave in the refrigerator until set. Serve with brown bread and butter.

# Potted Stilton

A very good way of using up Stilton. Cover with cling film.

**8 oz (225 g) Stilton cheese   2 oz (50 g) butter, softened
salt   a little port or Madeira**

Place the cheese in a bowl and mash thoroughly, then add butter and the salt and beat. Moisten with port or Madeira. Press into a small pot and if liked, melt a little extra butter and pour over to seal.

# Fresh Herb Cheese

Make a day in advance so that the herbs – parsley, chives, lemon thyme, marjoram – have time to flavour the cheese.

**8 oz (225 g) rich cream cheese
2 rounded tablespoons chopped fresh herbs
1 large clove garlic, crushed   single cream or top of milk
freshly ground black pepper   salt**

Place cheese in bowl with herbs and garlic. Beat well. Add cream or milk to mix to light cream. Season then turn into dish and chill. Keeps for up to 10 days in refrigerator, covered with cling film.

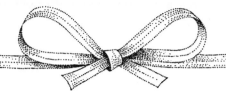

# Pork and Cranberry Terrine

*Serves 8*

This is a rich, slightly sweet terrine, which should be served cut in thick slices with lots of warm French bread or crusty rolls. Make in a foil loaf tin and take covered with cling film or foil and then it can be turned out on arrival. Eat the day after making.

**12 oz (350 g) stewing veal**
**12 oz (350 g) belly pork**
**12 oz (350 g) pig's liver    1 onion**
**1 clove garlic, crushed**
**2 teaspoons salt    freshly ground black pepper**
**2 tablespoons red wine**
**3 tablespoons cranberry sauce**
**8 rashers streaky bacon**

**1.** Heat the oven to 325 °F, 160°C, gas mark 3. Mince the veal, pork, liver and onion into a large bowl, add the garlic, salt, pepper, wine and cranberry sauce, and mix well.
**2.** Remove the rind from the bacon and use to line the base and sides of a 2 lb (900 g) loaf tin. Press in the meat mixture firmly, cover with foil and bake for 1¹/₂ hours. Remove from oven and discard the foil. Cover with a fresh piece and place weights or tins on top to press down firmly. When cold, refrigerate overnight. Will keep for 2-3 days in the refrigerator.

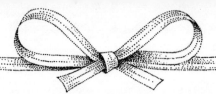

# Brandied Liver Pâté

*Serves 6*

A nice moist pâté, ideal to give as a present. Make it in a foil loaf tin and give the pâté in this.

**1 large onion, peeled and quartered
8 oz (225 g) chicken livers
8 oz (225 g) pork sausagemeat
3 tablespoons brandy
1 heaped tablespoon chopped parsley
1 level teaspoon salt    freshly ground black pepper
2 cloves garlic, crushed
about 5 rashers streaky bacon**

**1.** Purée the onion with the chicken livers. Add the sausagemeat, brandy, parsley, seasoning and garlic, and process until well mixed. Remove the rind and any bone from the bacon, and spread flat with a knife. Line the bottom and sides of a 1 lb (450 g) loaf tin with the rashers, put in the meat mixture and spread flat.
**2.** Cover the tin with foil, place in a roasting tin half filled with hot water, and cook at 325°F, 160°C, gas mark 3 for 1½ hours. The pâté is cooked if, when the centre is pierced with a skewer, the juices that run out are clear and it has slightly shrunk from the edges of the tin. Lightly weight the pâté with weights or tins on top. Leave to become quite cold. Will keep for 2-3 days in the refrigerator.

# Brittany Pâté

*Serves 6-8*

Make this in an inexpensive earthenware pâté dish and give it as part of the present too – or you could use a foil loaf tin.

**12 oz (350 g) pig's liver    1 small onion**
**8 oz (225 g) pork sausagemeat**
**½ level teaspoon salt    freshly ground black pepper**
**1½ level tablespoons freshly chopped mixed herbs**
**1 clove garlic**
**1 egg    2 bay leaves**
**5-6 rashers streaky bacon**

**1.** Heat the oven to 325°F, 160°C, gas mark 3. Mince the liver and onion into a bowl with the sausagemeat, seasoning, herbs, garlic and egg and mix well. Arrange the bay leaves in the bottom of a 1 lb (450 g) pâté dish or loaf tin.

**2.** Remove the rind and any bone from the bacon, smooth with the back of a knife and use to line the dish, making sure that the bay leaves stay in place. Press the meat mixture on top and smooth. Cover with a piece of foil. Place in a roasting tin half filled with hot water and cook for 1½ hours. The pâté is cooked when it has slightly shrunk from the sides of the dish and the juices run clear when the centre is pierced with a skewer. Remove from the oven and lightly weight the pâté with weights or tins. When quite cold chill in the refrigerator overnight. Will keep for 2-3 days in the refrigerator.

# CHILDREN

Children love giving presents. Encourage them to make their own for Mother's Day, Father's Day, family birthdays, as well as Christmas. Grandparents, godparents and favourite aunts all appreciate the personal touch and value the card the child has made and painted himself, however unskilfully, far more than an expensive one from a shop. And a tin of sticky toffee, a packet of irregular pieces of fudge, a box of oddly shaped biscuits bring far more pleasure than a box of chocolates from Harrods.

Children and sweets go together, so let them make their own. They can make a packing for their home-made toffee, decorate a plain box with drawings or make dolly bags from wrapping paper to fill with sweets or small biscuits.

Help the child, of course, but don't rush him. Let him think out what he is going to make, advise him if he asks, but *don't* do it for him.

It is an end of term tradition in a lot of schools to give small presents to the teacher, or even to one's best friend. Let the children give something they have made themselves.

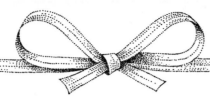

# Cornflake Crunchies

*Makes 18 cornflake crunchies*

Children enjoy making these. Use the other half egg in scrambled egg or to glaze a pastry pie.

**4 oz (100 g) soft margarine**
**3 oz (75 g) caster sugar**
**½ beaten egg**
**5 oz (150 g) self-raising flour**
**1 oz (25 g) cornflakes, lightly crushed**

**1.** Heat the oven to 375°F, 190°C, gas mark 5, and grease about 2 large baking sheets. Put the margarine into a large bowl, add the sugar, and cream together with a wooden spoon until soft. Beat in the egg, then slowly work in the flour until the mixture has come together. (If it is a warm day or the kitchen is hot the mixture may be rather soft to handle so wrap in cling film and chill for 10 minutes.)
**2.** Wet the hands and lightly roll the mixture into about 18 balls and then roll each in the crushed cornflakes. Place well spaced on the baking sheets and slightly flatten each with the hand. Bake for about 20-25 minutes until turning a very pale brown at the edges. Remove from the oven and leave on the trays for a minute before carefully lifting each biscuit onto a wire rack to cool. When cold store in an airtight tin until required.

# Caramel Krispies

*Makes about 34–40*

These would make a nice present, perhaps for class mates or teachers at the end of term. Best arranged in a single layer in a flat shallow box, then covered lightly with cling film.

**4 oz (100 g) hard margarine**
**4 oz (100 g) marshmallows**
**4 oz (100 g) caramels**
**7 oz (200 g) rice krispies**
**paper cake cases**

**1.** Put the margarine, marshmallows and caramels in a saucepan and heat gently over a moderate heat until the mixture is melted and smooth. Be patient, this will take about 5 minutes.
**2.** Meanwhile put the rice krispies in a large bowl. Remove the pan from the heat and pour all at once onto the rice krispies and stir very thoroughly until they are well and evenly coated. Spoon into paper cake cases, as much or as little as you like! Leave in a cool place until set and firm.

# No Cook Fudge

*Makes 36 squares*

Children love to make this, and the only difficult part lies in persuading them to leave the fudge to harden overnight. Pack in small plastic bags, tied with a ribbon, or if making the mice they are best carefully arranged in a single layer in a box.

**6 oz (175 g) butter**
**1 small can sweetened condensed milk**
**1 lb, 12 oz (800 g) icing sugar, sieved**

Cream the butter in a bowl until soft and then stir in the condensed milk. Now gradually add the icing sugar and when all is worked in, turn onto a work surface lightly sprinkled with icing sugar and knead until smooth. Roll out to ½ inch (1.25 cm) thickness and cut into neat squares. Leave to harden overnight on a wire rack covered with a clean muslin or tea towel.

## VARIATIONS

*Sultana fudge.* Add about 4 oz (100 g) roughly chopped sultanas to the basic mixture and knead until evenly distributed.
*Chocolate.* Sieve 3 oz (75 g) cocoa with the icing sugar and make as above.
*Peppermint mice.* Add a few drops of peppermint essence to the basic mixture. Break off into small pieces and shape into mice (about 12). Use currants for the eyes, coloured balls for a nose, angelica for whiskers and flaked almonds for ears.

# Mallow Tiffin

*Makes 16 pieces of tiffin*

Always popular and easy for the children to make themselves. Snip the marshmallows with scissors dipped in water. Arrange in a box, cover with cling film and decorate with a ribbon or string.

**4 oz (100 g) hard margarine**
**3 level tablespoons golden syrup**
**1 oz (25 g) drinking chocolate**
**2 oz (50 g) marshmallows, snipped in small pieces**
**8 oz (225 g) digestive biscuits, crushed**

**TOPPING**
**6 oz (175 g) plain or milk chocolate**

**1.** Line a shallow 7 × 11 inch (17.5 × 27.5 cm) tin with foil. Place the margarine, syrup and drinking chocolate in a pan and heat until the butter has melted. Remove from the heat and cool slightly, then stir in the marshmallows and biscuits (if the mixture is too warm the marshmallows melt). Mix thoroughly and then turn into the tin, press down firmly and refrigerate until firm.
**2.** Break the chocolate into small pieces and place in a bowl over a pan of hot water until melted, then spread over the biscuit base and leave until set. Peel off the foil and cut the tiffin into 16 pieces.

# Chocolate Chip Drops

*Makes about 34 chocolate chip drops*

These are an ideal gift for children to make when a visit to Granny is imminent, and they are only too happy to help eat them up! Best packed in a plastic bag firmly tied with ribbon.

**4 oz (100 g) soft margarine**
**2 oz (50 g) caster sugar**
**2 oz (50 g) soft brown sugar**
**1 egg, beaten**
**6 oz (175 g) self-raising flour**
**6 oz (175 g) chocolate chips**

**1.** Heat the oven to 350°F, 180°C, gas mark 4. Well grease 3 baking sheets. Place the margarine, sugars, egg and flour in a bowl and beat well together, until thoroughly blended. Stir in the chocolate chips.
**2.** Place the mixture in teaspoonfuls well spaced on the baking sheets. Bake in the oven for about 10 minutes or until a pale golden brown. Leave to cool on the baking sheets for 2 minutes and then leave to cool on a wire rack. Store in an airtight tin.

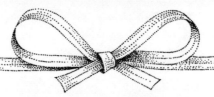

# Pomander

*Makes 1 pomander*

Not really food, except that it is made from things in the kitchen. Children like to make pomanders for grandparents. Tie pretty ribbons or cord around the orange so that they can be hung up in the wardrobe, or cupboard.

**1 medium orange**
**enough cloves to cover, approximately 2 oz (50 g)**
**½ teaspoon mixed spice**
**½ teaspoon cinnamon**

**1.** Press the cloves into the orange so that it is completely covered. Mix the spices together and roll the orange in them.
**2.** Leave to dry in a warm place such as an airing cupboard for 3-4 weeks until dried out. Decorate as required.

# SPECIAL PRESENTS

You have been invited to stay with friends and you want to say thank-you. This is the time for a very special present. In the luxury class would be a joint of really prime beef (rare enough in the average household these days) or a bacon or gammon joint that you have cooked and glazed yourself. Take the present with you – but do let your hostess know in advance what you are bringing.

You might like to take a side of smoked salmon, a few smoked trout. Or take a dish already frozen for your hostess's freezer – after first making sure that she has room to accommodate it.

At Christmas a jar of brandy butter, or a special turkey stuffing will be welcome, or you could take a tin of mince pies or a pudding. For an Easter weekend or a summer visit there could be a raised pie, or a cold roast capon to be eaten with salad and a bottle of your home-made mayonnaise to go with it.

# Turkey Stuffing

Enough to stuff a 14 lb (6.3 kg) turkey. Make these the day before needed. Wrap in cling film, ready to go into the bird on Christmas morning.

### CHESTNUT STUFFING WITH WATERCRESS

**1 lb, 15 oz (880 g) can whole chestnuts in water**
**8 oz (225 g) streaky bacon, chopped**
**2 oz (50 g) butter**
**4 oz (100 g) fresh brown breadcrumbs**
**1 egg, beaten   1 bunch watercress, finely chopped**
**1 tablespoon caster sugar**
**2 teaspoons salt   ground black pepper**

**1.** Drain the liquid from the chestnuts and turn them into a bowl. Gently mash with a fork to break into small chunky pieces. Fry the bacon slowly to let the fat run out and then increase the heat and fry quickly until crisp. Lift out with a slotted spoon and add to the chestnuts.
**2.** Add the butter to the pan and allow to melt, then add the breadcrumbs and fry until brown; turn into the bowl. Add the remaining ingredients and mix very thoroughly. Use to stuff the body cavity of the turkey.

## SAUSAGE, LEMON AND THYME STUFFING

**1 oz (25 g) butter    1 onion, chopped**
**1 lb (450 g) pork sausagemeat**
**4 oz (100 g) fresh white breadcrumbs**
**grated rind and juice of 1 lemon**
**1 level teaspoon salt    ground black pepper**
**2 tablespoons chopped parsley**
**1 level teaspoon fresh thyme or ½ teaspoon dried thyme**

Melt the butter, add the onion and fry gently until soft. Stir in the remaining ingredients and mix well. Use to stuff the breast of the turkey.

# Raised Chicken and Egg Pie

*Serves 8*

A special present that is perfect to take when you are going to spend a long weekend with friends. Wrap in cling film to transport it.

3½ lb (1.5 kg) chicken
8 oz (225 g) streaky bacon, minced or chopped
1 tablespoon chopped fresh herbs
2 teaspoons salt, according to saltiness of the bacon
ground black pepper
6 small hard-boiled eggs, shelled
beaten egg to glaze

PASTRY
12 oz (350 g) plain flour
1 teaspoon salt
5 oz (150 g) lard
¼ pint (150 ml) water, plus 2 tablespoons

**1.** Grease a 7 inch (17.5 cm) loose-bottomed cake tin. First carve the leg and thigh off the chicken, then remove the skin and bone. Take the meat off the rest of the bird, discard the skin and make stock from the bones. Cube all the chicken meat and put in a bowl with the bacon, herbs and seasoning.

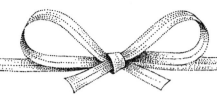

**2.** Now make the pastry. Put the flour and salt into a bowl, put the lard and water into a pan and allow the lard to melt and the water to boil. Make a well in the centre of the flour and pour on all the liquid, mixing quickly with a wooden spoon or fork until it becomes a smooth dough. When it is cool enough to handle, take two-thirds of the dough and roll into a circle 3 inches (7.5 cm) larger than the tin. Slip this into the tin and with the hands work it evenly up the sides until it comes to the top of the tin.

**3.** Put half the chicken mixture in the tin, and level it. Make 6 dents in the mixture and arrange the eggs in them. Cover with remaining meat mixture and flatten.

**4.** Brush inside top of the pastry case with beaten egg. Roll out the remaining pastry to a circle just over 7 inches (17.5 cm) for the lid and lift on top of the pie, press edges firmly together and flute using the thumb and first finger of the right hand and the index finger of the left hand. Make four holes in the centre of the pie and if liked decorate with pastry leaves. Brush with beaten egg and bake in the oven at 425°F, 220°C, gas mark 7 for 45 minutes. Reduce the heat to 350°F, 180°C, gas mark 4 for a further 30 minutes. Remove from the oven and leave to cool in the tin. Chill overnight before turning out and serving with salads.

# Brandy Butter

*Makes about 1 lb (450 g)*

Brandy butter to serve with mince pies and Christmas pudding is always a very acceptable gift. Pack in small glasses or jars, cover with cling film and label neatly.

**8 oz (225 g) unsalted butter, softened**
**8 oz (225 g) icing sugar, sieved**
**about 6 tablespoons brandy**

Cream the butter with a wooden spoon until soft and then beat in the icing sugar. Continue beating until the mixture is light and fluffy, then beat in the brandy. It is a good idea to pack the brandy butter into the jars, glasses or containers for giving at this stage as it is soft and easy to manage. Keep in the refrigerator until required.

## CUMBERLAND RUM BUTTER

Make as above but without the brandy and then add grated orange rind with a little lemon juice and mix thoroughly. Add just sufficient rum to flavour well. The butter will have a rum flavour with a good tang of orange and makes a nice change with Christmas puddings.

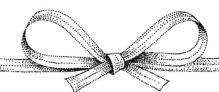

# Glazed Gammon

*Serves 8*

A very special gift. When cold place the gammon on a paper or foil plate, put parsley around the bottom and then cover with cling film. Will keep in the refrigerator for up to 1 week or freeze for up to a month.

**3 lb (1.4 kg) boned gammon joint**

**GLAZE**
**2 teaspoons dry mustard**
**1 oz (25 g) demerara sugar    1 tablespoon honey**

**DECORATION**
**cloves    maraschino cherries    cocktail sticks**

**1.** Soak the gammon overnight in cold water, then drain and dry. Check its weight, place on a piece of foil and then wrap like a parcel. Allow 45 minutes to the lb (450 g) and bake at 375°F, 190°C, gas mark 5.
**2.** Mix together the ingredients for the glaze, and, 30 minutes before the end of the cooking time, remove the gammon from the oven. Open the foil and pour off the juices (these are very good used up in soups). Remove the rind and score the fat in a diamond pattern. Press the glaze over the fat and return to the oven for the last 30 minutes, with the foil open to allow the fat to brown. Baste with the glaze. Leave to become cold, then put a clove on the end of half a cocktail stick, spear through a cherry and place one in each diamond.

# Real Home–made Mayonnaise

*Makes about 1¹/₄ pints (750ml)*

A gift that is especially suitable for a gourmet friend who has no time to make any. As a variation add a little chopped chives or tarragon to the finished mayonnaise. Place in an attractive glass jar, which can be part of the gift.

**2 eggs   1 teaspoon salt**
**plenty of ground black pepper**
**scant teaspoon made mustard**
**1 teaspoon caster sugar**
**1 tablespoon wine or cider vinegar**
**1 pint (600 ml) oil (2 parts corn to 1 part olive oil)**
**juice of 1 lemon**

Place all the ingredients except the oil and lemon juice in a processor or blender and process for a few moments. Keep the processor switched on, then add the oil in a slow steady stream until all has been added. The mayonnaise will now be thick. Add the lemon juice and process again. Taste and check seasoning. Put in small jars, label, and store in the refrigerator for up to 1 month.

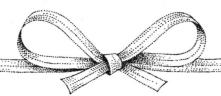

# Home Salted Nuts

Almonds, Brazils or cashews can all be prepared like this and make a delicious present. Pack in very small wooden bowls and give as part of the present, or use small see-through bags with labels.

To each 2 oz (50 g) nuts add:

**1 oz (25 g) butter**
**1 teaspoon corn oil**
**a little salt**

**1.** If necessary blanch the nuts to remove the outer skins.
**2.** Heat the butter and oil in a frying pan, add the nuts and fry over a moderate heat, turning constantly until golden brown all over. Lift out with a slotted spoon and drain on kitchen paper. Sprinkle with salt.

# THE THOUGHT THAT COUNTS

In the end it is the thought that has gone into your food present that matters, the care that you have taken in choosing and presenting it.

A good present is a hamper or basket with an exciting selection of delicious things packed into it. This is great fun to plan – and to receive. It can cost a lot or a little, can be elaborate or simple. Plan it very thoughtfully. You can mix home-made and bought food. Include something that the recipient cannot often afford – a Stilton perhaps, or a farmhouse Cheddar, fresh butter, a few expensive chocolates, a really good tea, or special canned goods that the ordinary person does not normally buy, a rich fruit cake.

Jars or tins of layered dried fruits and nuts would appeal to someone who likes health foods. You might even make up a special health-food hamper. You could include small home-made gingham bags of peppercorns, bayleaves, or dried herbs from your own garden, labelled accordingly.

The simplest ideas are often the most effective. A friend living in town will be overjoyed with a small wicker basket of fresh brown country eggs, packed in authentic straw, with a few hen's feathers. She can use the basket later for fruit or bread.

A basket piled high with satsumas and decorated with a few leaves, if possible, will please a friend living alone. For gourmets there could be a small basket of the more exotic fruits like mangoes, lichees, kiwi fruit, a small Ogen melon.

Baskets of your own fresh vegetables can go to friends who do not garden, and your own freshly baked loaf or small rolls to those who do not cook.

Before you pack a basket for a friend in hospital do make sure that edible presents are allowed. Hospital diet can be monotonous and something to tempt the patient's appetite is what you should aim at. Fruit is nearly always popular. If you give sweets make them light and refreshing rather than sweet and sticky, not chocolate but fruit bonbons attractively packaged. Most sick people like a lot of fruit drinks, so include if you can a bottle or two of your home-made lemonade.

You will of course dress up your hospital present as prettily as you can and add a posy of fresh flowers with your get well card.

Finally there are the tools of the trade. A selection of small kitchen tools need not cost a lot – a small non-stick saucepan, for instance, a really sharp kitchen knife, a special potato peeler or a garlic press – tie on a big bow and give it with your love. All cooks, aspiring or expert, are fascinated by presents like these.

# INDEX